Also by Ron Butlin

FICTION
The Sound of My Voice
Night Visits
The Tilting Room
Vivaldi and the Number 3
Belonging
No More Angels
Ghost Moon

POETRY
The Wonnerfu Warld o John Milton
Stretto
Creatures Tamed by Cruelty
The Exquisite Instrument
Ragtime in Unfamiliar Bars
Histories of Desire
Without a Backward Glance
The Magicians of Edinburgh

DRAMA
We've Been Had
Blending In
Sweet Dreams

OPERA LIBRETTI
Markheim
Dark Kingdom
Faraway Pictures
Good Angel, Bad Angel
The Perfect Woman
The Money Man
Wedlock

Ron Butlin
The Magicians of Scotland

RECENT POETRY

with drawings by
JAMES HUTCHESON

Polygon

First published in Great Britain in 2015
by Polygon,
an imprint of Birlinn Ltd

West Newington House
10 Newington Road
Edinburgh
EH9 1QS

www.polygonbooks.co.uk

ISBN 9781846972911

British Library Cataloguing-in-Publication Data
A catalogue record for this book is available on request
from the British Library.

Book design and drawings
© James Hutcheson
Typeset in 10/14pt Veridgris MVB

Printed and bound
by TJ International Ltd, Padstow, Cornwall

The publishers acknowledge investment from Creative Scotland

Contents

Acknowledgements

Grateful thanks are due to the editors of the following publications where some of the poems first appeared: *The Stinging Fly* (Eire), *World Literature Today* (USA), *Herald*, *Scottish Review of Books*, *Gutter*, *Atlanta Review* (USA), *Perspectives*, *Scotsman*, *Neu! Reekie! #UntitledOne*. Some were contained in *Without a Backward Glance* (Barzan Publishing) or broadcast on BBC Radio 4 and 5. Several of the poems have been jazzed up by Dick Lee for *Edinburgh Science*, *Edinburgh Magic*, *A Very Edinburgh Celebration* and *Edinburgh Lily* on the Edinburgh Fringe 2013-15. Also for *The Games* which was first performed by the jazz ensemble Dr Lee's Prescription, at the Glasgow Commonwealth Games in 2014.

The author appreciates the commissioning of some poems by the Edinburgh UNESCO City of Literature, City of Edinburgh Council, Authors Reading Festival, *Look Up Edinburgh* (Freight Publications), Scottish Opera, Authors' Licensing and Collection Society. In company with many other Scottish writers, he would like to acknowledge the unfailing kindness and support of the late Gavin Wallace.

Ron Butlin would like to thank Creative Scotland for a Professional Development grant which allowed him to complete *The Magicians of Scotland*.

Dedication

To my wife Regi, Dick Lee and Anne Evans
– magicians all!

MAGIC PLACES

*Though brought up in a very small Borders village, I have lived
mostly in cities here and abroad. Like much of modern life, my
longing to return to village life is untested, and fairly suspect.*

The Electric City of Heck

Cattle stumbling their way down to the shallows.
The water's coolness rising
To meet them. Their hooves dry and hard
Against a clatter of loose stones *etc.* . . . .

Having rusted not quite closed,
The sluice gate's cast-iron lip runs
With several downward streaks
Of wet sunlight *etc.* . . . .

Brushstrokes painted on a long-ago afternoon,
And erased –
The strands of current drift midstream,
Their several interlocking patterns describe . . .

Etc. etc. etc. . . . .

*

Isn't it time I trashed such childhood fancies?
After all, I live in the electric city
and the electric city lives in me.
My pulse is the traffic's stop-and-go.

What I know of love and friendship
naming the only streets I care for.

So . . . ?

How come I keep helter-skeltering back to – where?

And for what?

To give the supermarket checkout,
aisles and shelves a *pastoral* makeover –
smothering them in flowers, weeds
and a purple sway of willow herb?
Scythe down a field of business magnates,
bankers and politicians (row upon sleek row
baled and stacked, ready
to be recycled into something useful)?

Hardly. And yet . . .

Almost overnight, our city's been digitised,
uploaded to an encrypted site / its inhabitants
given new user names,
new passwords.

Our histories deleted at a mouse-click
everyone's now making up the truth.

Beneath a touchscreen sky of low-watt
urban stars we continue our separate journeys

from the very centre of the universe
(where all our journeys start from, especially
the most personal).

We share nothing. The name for our loneliness
is self. We live for moments of recognition,
for brief communion.

*

Accelerating away from the Lockerbie bombing –

Staying a decade and more clear of the Twin Towers –

Keeping the next atrocity always
a few days ahead –

Gaza, Syria, Afghanistan, Iraq and all the rest
are parked in a layby for the time being
(with luck, a tow-truck might be
on its way).

Same road, same destination.

Still *en route* to where we're always making for –
you, me and the memories we rely on
like outdated maps ...

*

Or else, should I return to that summer's afternoon?
Rebrand it: *The Electric City of Heck.*
#solidground.

Upgrade its farm and half-dozen cottages (built mostly
from the rubble of nearby Lochmaben Castle).
Reformat it for the 21st century into:

- A glass cathedral that promises unlimited FaceTime
  between Man and his God of choice
- A glacier's permafrost to slow the seasons' meltdown
- An ocean, cleansed to offer us all a second chance

Then, if all else fails –

Taking the best of what we have and the best
of what we are, let's reconfigure:

a streamlined rush of swifts that eat, sleep
and mate on the wing,
never touching the Earth from here
to Africa.
Not angels, but our guides into
a trackless future –

our guides, our inspiration.

Skara Brae in Orkney is the oldest known settlement in Britain.
A visit there can be a truly moving experience, especially if the
weather is at its rawest. It was hidden under sand dunes until a
storm cleared these away in 1850.

Disposable Buildings Are Made For Disposable Lives

It seems the likes of you and me will always fail
to keep to IKEA's clearly-arrowed pathways,
ending up homeless among glassware,
candles, pin boards, towels,
closely-planted wardrobes.

When we come to a lake of stranded beds,
we know we're lost. And so –
it's back to the kitchens that cannot cook,
to the playrooms whose primary-coloured brightness
hurts us with remembrance.

Passing through unnoticed, we leave no trace.

When did our weatherless, windowless,
prefabricated hours become
whole days, whole months,
whole years?
When did we mislay the lives we *meant* to lead?
Settling, instead, for flat-packed dreams, for hopes
more easily expressed as trends

in bathroom furniture?

*

500 years before we built the Great Pyramid of Cheops,
5,000 years before we built IKEA,
Orkney men, women and children
carried back-breaking weights
of stone. They split them,
trimmed them to exact size, chiselled
to confirm a perfect fit,
then placed them.

The scouring wind showed where.

Skara Brae, the Knap of Howar.

*

IKEA bricks and breeze blocks will soon
come tumbling down. That deepest blue
industrial-scale sheeting
(what we've learned to call 'sky'),
will drift elsewhere.

One day, our line of sight will clear.
It always does. To show us:

Winter 1850. Bay of Skaill.
The worst storm in living memory –

Arctic winds batter sea and shore, hacking
at Orkney *machair* and dunes until
the weighted veil of several
thousand years' sand is
finally lifted . . .

Revealing –

This stone-slabbed dresser, this bed, this hearth.
Eight dwellings in all, a network
of connecting passages.

This human warren.

Home.

I had the honour to be Edinburgh's Makar / Poet Laureate from 2008-14. Sadly, all good things must come to an end.

Edinburgh Doesn't Scan That Easy

Six years I tried to turn our city into rhyme –
I listened to its heartbeat, pulse . . .
and time after time after time
my too-poetic stress was out of sync.

Edinburgh doesn't scan that easy. You think.
You plan. Pen, paper, make a start –
but our city's all-too-wayward heart
just batters on, no matter what you say.

Thanks to high finance, the homeless in the malls,
the pubs, drugs, the tourists, and festivals
running night and day –
our streets have learned to stray.
Buildings never stay where they've been put,
tram tracks come and go, *ditto*
banks and parliaments. Consultants who compute
our futures always get them wrong.

And so . . .

As one, the public clocks will whirr and chime,
bursting into song!
Rush-hour men and women heel-kick, dance –

they finger-click the city beat,
its commerce and romance
from Leith to Arthur's Seat!

I stand on North Bridge gazing east and west –
the distant Forth, the Gardens, galleries, the sky.
A train comes rumbling out of Waverley . . .

This I take on trust, and all the rest.

✦

The laurel crown, the Council Makar cape and quill
are each invisible,
likewise the laureate whose term is done.
Time to take my leave, time to hand them on . . .

Leuchars railway station, on the line between Edinburgh and
Dundee, is a place where time often seems to have stopped. Forever.

Rehearsals for The End Of Time

Room heaters switched off, and all lights.
Doors locked, steel shutters pulled down,
benches removed. Arctic winds and
North Sea sleet scour every surface
of its history.

No pyramids, no Renaissance,
no rise and fall of mighty empires –
not now. Not ever.
Only this battened-down brickwork. Only me
going nowhere.

I'm sure it was a summer's day when I came across
the metal footbridge. I remember sunlight.
Mid-January now by the feel of it,
and the clock's hands stuck
at a quarter-past ten . . .

(Once upon a time I lived in the warm hills
above Barcelona,
I'd stroll each evening beneath shower upon
shower of falling stars. So many wishes to make,
so many lifetimes to look forward to . . .)

These are Scottish stars hammered
into east coast darkness,
right up to the hilt.
Bringing the Cosmic Wheel to a standstill.

An RAF jet hangs silent and motionless 100ft or so
above platform 2 –
had it been planning to liberate someone,
somewhere? Was it en *route* to yet another country
to help them become
just like us?

No train in sight, nor hope of any.

Rehearsals for the End of Time
take place, it seems,
here at Leuchars station.

As a small boy, I was taken to see Edinburgh's last tram trundle its final journey along Princes Street before being scrapped. The rails were tarmacked over. Less than fifty years later, the pollution and traffic jams had become so bad it was proposed to re-lay the tracks. These poems can be seen on the timetable for each stop.

Stations of the Rush Hour

YORK PLACE

First stop on the line, or the last?
Into the future, or out of the past?
We get on, we get off – that's all we can know
for our journey started long, long ago.

ST ANDREW'S SQUARE

Scotland, too, is a green island. Here
we're hemmed in by cliffs of sheerest glass
and heavy-duty stonework.
Time to make waves
as we sail this Tarmac-Black Sea!

PRINCES STREET

WARNING – the budget allowed for one stop only
along the entire length of our capital's main street.

Make the most of it!

WEST END

If there's time before your tram, enjoy this pause
in the city's hustle-bustle, push-and-press.
Let the sky, the trees and the pleasing
curve of Atholl Crescent soothe
your downtown stress . . .

HAYMARKET

Nearby, five roads meet and snarl and clash (traffic-
tangles, red lights, criss-cross lanes and criss-
cross drivers), while we go two-rail smoothly
gliding past.

MURRAYFIELD

Even when the pitch and seats are empty,
a hushed roar fills the stadium –

Let's hear it loud enough for Scotland!

BALGREEN

Beware that nearby block of bricked-up darkness,
the JENNERS DEPOSITORY!
You'll hear tales of locks, bolts
and security, tales of storage –
long-term *personal* storage.

Best to pray your tram's already on its way . . .

SAUGHTON

Here the tram grows up into an adult train, running
on the straight and narrow. Citywards it goes
to seek its fortune . . .
and then returns, urged on by the winds
of change, the winds of opportunity.
Always the wind, the wind,
the wind . . .

BANKHEAD

Work? Study? Here's where to come!
You can Makro and Screwfix, Parcel and Plumb.
When the buying and selling and learning are done,
clamber aboard and sit yourself down . . .
You can rest, for soon you'll be home.

EDINBURGH PARK STATION

CUT-PRICE! DISCOUNT! SALES!
You're loaded up with bargains?
Stay upon the rails!

Home by car or tram or train or bus?
The choice is surely obvious!
Why busy-station, traffic-jam it,
when you can easy-glide, and tram it!

EDINBURGH PARK CENTRAL

Glass hillsides line this sober business glen.
Come summer, there'll be picnic-ceilidhs when
Diageo gets frisky
– and turns the waterfall to whisky!

GYLE CENTRAL

Let's stop and shop a while.
No lifeless mouse-click screens. Here's REAL!
Real shops, real people,
a mall that has real style.
Cash or card, and service with a smile!

GOGARBURN (*for* RBS)

A magic wand created these glass-and-mirror palaces
out of reflected cloud and sky, like money itself
created out of nothing but
human trust – and without it, everything is lost,
including us.

INGLISTON

Park it / Lock it / Leave it.
No traffic mess, no stress. Believe it!
Be a rush-hour loafer –
here's your tram, your chauffeur!

AIRPORT

The first stop, and the last –
the future begins . . .
and so does the past.

If you've just landed here on Earth,
then welcome!
If you're about to leave us – safe return!

In 2004 Edinburgh sent a delegation to Brussels. They returned the same day, the capital of Scotland having been designated the world's first UNESCO City of Literature.

What the Well-Dressed City Wears

Feeling good after a spot of devolution,
our country's capital hung up
its pressed-tight, three-piece suit,
kicked off its brick-thick brogues
(the ones with business

toecaps) and, lighter now by several centuries,
hopped . . .
   skipped . . .
      and jumped
(the Castle . . .
          Calton Hill . . .
              and Leith)
across to EuroLand.

Bureaucratic blessing! Same-day turnaround!

Back home to Scottish rain that runs to
      whisky faster than
   it's poured . . .

New-named, new-branded Edinburgh will cut
its own imaginary cloth
out of nothing,
trimming for a perfect fit.

Now on you go, Auld Reekie! Strut
your literary stuff around the globe –

wearing the miracle of words, and nothing but!

The Ninth Roman Legion invaded Scotland c120AD, and was never seen again. It was all so very, very long ago, and yet ...

The Roman Invasion of Scotland

Thanks to the ruler-straight road from here to Rome
and back again, we saw them coming miles away.

Call up the bards to verse and curse!
Druids to stop the clocks, freeze-frame
the weather, make screen-shots of the day
ten cohorts of six hundred men
came clambering over the Wall.

That was the Roman invasion of Scotland,
the one and only.

2,000 years on they're still here, still wandering
the Celtic mist, still taking wrong turns
on the wrong tracks in the long-gone
Forest of Caledon.

For them, it's a late November afternoon,
and always will be. Darkness falling,
night ahead, and always,
always raining.

Sinister ... dexter / Sinister ... dexter ...

*

The Pentland Hills in summer –
a cloud passing over the sun.
Sudden chill. Sudden skirl of sleet
from an empty sky.

Here they come – IX Legio Hispana!

So worn-out now. So skin-and-bone weightless.
Their buckles, belts and body-armour
tattered air; their shields
and swords trails of rust . . .
We watch them march march
march across Flotterstone Water
making hardly a ripple.

(Not the sort of invasions we view on YouTube –
Blockbuster wars with blockbuster budgets!
SHOCK AND AWE, and the sequel
OPERATION ENDURING FREEDOM
with its drones, its jets,
its PR threats –
all for $77 billion.
Tomahawk missiles at $1 million *per*,
delivering freedom and democracy . . .)

Sinister . . .dexter / Sinister . . . dexter . . .

*

Look close. How many lifetimes does it take
to read what's right before our very eyes?
Pictish runes, sprayed graffiti,
hidden landmines . . .

The future's scripted everywhere around us –

Carefully then, so very carefully, let's brush aside
these last few grains of sand . . .

*

One day soon (give or take a million years),
Scald Law and Carnethy will have levelled down
to folded layers of white-heat, seared-red
rock that ebbs and flows,
cooling to form its new geology –
ancient lives and ours long gone.

The Pentlands freeze over. The cold sun
barely risen, makes evening shadows
of all that has been said and done.

Sinister . . . dexter / Sinister . . . dexter. . .

This set of poems celebrates the Glasgow Commonwealth Games 2014, the athletes and some of their countries, and was performed there with jazz band Dr Lee's Prescription.

The Commonwealth Games

1. STARTING THE RACE

Starts with a breath

Deep breath and again

Muscle and mind, tension and strain.

Breathe in, breathe deep,
breathe, breathe,
breathe till you keep

your muscle, keep your mind, keep
keep, keep your muscle,
your mind, your soul poised
as one –

for the race was begun
a long time ago.

*

And so –

you are here. And so
you are now.

And *this* is the here –

This is the now . . .

The briefest split-second to go,
time starts to slow . . .

Your muscles, your mind, your soul start to flow
into each other,
                    and all
        into *this* –

The bliss of the perfect, the moment . . .

                            The bliss
                of the race . . .
        beginning . . .

NOW!!!

2. AFRICA

Once was dark,
was darkness –
blazing into light!

Light trance, light born,
life dance, life song –

YES, dance! YES, dance!
YES!

Sing the roads and rivers,
Sing the tracks and trails.

Sing Sahara sandstorms
YES!

Sing skies and grasslands,
lakes and shore.
Continent a song, a dance floor –

Bless the dancers and their dance as one!
Bless the singers who become
their song –

YES, dance! YES, dance!
YES!

Sing fast-money, sing fast cities,
dance the township home,

Rainbow-shimmer, cascade roar,
Shining, shining as never before!

YES!

Sing the street, the beat,
the heart, the heat –

where rhythm's king
till Kingdom Come!

YES! Dance. YES! Dance.
YES!

3. RUNNING THE RACE

Silence . . .
Not a sigh, not a word, not a –
Sssh!

Stillness . . .
          stilled breath
     . . . stilled body
before . . .
          the pistol is raised –
       before . . .
the pistol. . .
          is steadied . . .
       is fired!

Wired,
       inspired,
              and all at once done –

The race has begun!

*

Regions, countries
stripped down for speed –

All rushing forward,
all for the need

to go and keep going –

Fast from the block,
fast on the straight,

fast on the curve –

faster the muscle,
faster the nerve,

straining, gaining . . .

Stride and feel
toe-stamp and heel
turning the track –

turning the earth!

Spikes digging deep,
to keep the earth turned

to the beat of their hearts,
to the heat of their blood.

The race is the start
and the end of it all –

Body and mind, spirit and soul.

Moment of wholencss –

Moment of grace –

THE RACE! THE RACE! THE RACE!

4. INDIA (RAGA)

Brahmaputra, Dhaleswari, Kushiyara, Kalcodonga
Punpun, Damra,
Punpun, Darma...

Bamba Dhura, Chandrashila,
Kalanag, Nanda Khat,
Kalanag, Bama Dhur...

Mentok, Mentok, Nag Tibba,
Mentok, Mentok, Nag Tibba...

Uttar Pradesh, Madhya Pradesh
Odisha, Orissa, Bihar, Rhajasthan...

Gujarat, Goa, Assam,
Gujarat, Goa, Assam...

Amril, Amni, Anand,
Baddi, Baruch, Baruch
Amril, Amni, Anand...

Etawa, Dhampur, Etawa, Dhampur,

Gaya, Gaya, Jalna, Kanda,
Gaya, Gaya, Katni, Kanda,

Gaya, Gaya, Gaya...

5. CARIBBEAN

The downtown street's a reggae beat,
Sun-island melting sugar-sweet.
Blue water sky, clam-coral sea,
Reggae is king, reggae is free!

No master, no slave, no more –
History's sand blowing the shore,
history's wind criss-crossing the cane,
master / slave all over again . . .

But not on these islands, not in these seas
where the reggae beat heartbeat's
shaking the trees,
where traffic goes offbeat rhythm to please
the dancer, romancer, financer
and chancer taking their ease
at ninety degrees
in the shade.

They've all got it made!

*

The downtown street's a reggae beat,
Sun-island melting sugar-sweet.
Blue-water sky, clam-coral sea,
Reggae is king, reggae is free!

6. AUSTRALIA (DREAMTIME)

ROO, OZ, OZ, ROO –
Didgery – Didgery –
Didgerydoo!

OZ, ROO, ROO, OZ –
Because . . .

Red rock core, sun-crazed heart,
hollowed-out sun-blazed art.

Breathless birth to dreamless death,
breath that never stops for breath.

Heat to seize and squeeze the trees,
bursting seed to flame –
to live and die,
and live again.

OZ, ROO, ROO, OZ –
Always is, always was.

Past's a dream we've slept right through,

Present's what we've woken to.

ROO, OZ, OZ, ROO!
The future's coming true!

7. GLASGOW

Constructing the seven seas,
welding the world together –

Clyebuilt hulls.
Clydebuilt plates and rivets.
Bulwarks, bulkheads,
gangways, decks.

Constructing the five continents,
binding capital to capital,
country to country –

Springburn locomotives,
Springburn couplings, cabs,
smokestacks, pistons, valves.

Steam City, Power City,
Iron and Girder City!

Dockyards, rails, slipways, foundries.
John Brown's, Fairfield,
the Finnieston Crane!

Built the world once, and will build it again!

*

Blasted clean of smoke and grime –
New City, Now City!
Sky-scraping Glass-and-Mirror City!

Roads that rush and . . .
                    swerve and . . .
                                soar!
Till far and near are curves of air.

Circle within Circle – descend
deep down . . .
                and rise!
Always, always rise!

Futures bought and futures sold
on a million . . .
                billion . . . .
                            trillion
electronic pathways.

New City! Now City!

Global City Glasgow!

Though born in Edinburgh, I spent much of my twenties
and thirties drifting here and there across the globe, all very
pleasurably. It wasn't until I stood in the Calvinist grip
of a Scottish winter's afternoon that I at last accepted my
Scottishness. Since then I have rejoiced in it!

Near Linton Burnfoot

Tarred roads, metal cattle-grids and wheel tracks mesh
so tightly no land can escape. Tractor ruts
cut deep into the grass to cross and double-stitch
the fields together. Where the high ground pushes upwards,
pylons rigid with electricity stand guard
upon the hills. Bridges staple running water,
lines of fence-posts nail the valley sides in place.

Rain and ploughed mud. Rooks' cries claw the air,
a *banshee* trapped in corrugated iron shrieks
to be released. Trees grasp at nothing,
and let go. It is a scene a child has painted,
splashing colours on sodden paper:
his carelessness might tear a mountainside apart.

Shingle being ground to nothing on the river-bed,
the clouds' silence soaking into the hills –
these are secrets I dare not tell
even to myself. They give weight
to every moment of my life.

MAGIC PEOPLE

Having sulked in Loch Ness for centuries, would Nessie have welcomed the recent referendum?

The Loch Ness Monster's Post-referendum Curse

Behold my northern stretch of sullen, sunless
rock-hard, wind-scarred, rain-lashed cold,
cold water. My dark-fathomed kingdom,
my home.

They hauled me up from the depths –
for a photo-op!

They websited me!
Facebooked me!
YouTubed my coils!

A Profile on LinkedIn I was supposed to complete!
Me? . . .

    Me? . . .

        Me . . . whose hundred-year, thousand-year
roar could have battle cry-ed our nation –

and they wanted me to tweet?

*

Now they've had their referendum,
I'll download the lot –

Then DELETE, DELETE, DELETE!

Towards the end of his life the Polish composer Chopin [1810-49] visited Edinburgh, staying briefly in Stockbridge. He was already in very poor health.

Frédéric Chopin Tweets from the Edinburgh Hogmanay Party

A year before he died, Frédéric Chopin stood outside
his Stockbridge flat and looked up
at the stars.

Could the pull of their distant gravities restore his–?

Next moment (feet hardly touching the cobbles,
Georgian elegance shuddering in his slipstream),
he's accelerating 150 years and more
into the future.

Blurring past lanes that fist staccato-
hammered *scherzos*,
past railings that finger-click *mazurkas*,
past clubs, boutiques and basement bars
going into meltdown.

Edinburgh's skyline cascades upwards as a rushed
arpeggio of slate and sunlight.

*

Arriving at Princes Street in time to catch
the last few minutes of the last day
of 2013.

So many men, so many women. Hundreds
of them, thousands of them, standing room only.
Day-Glo security, barricades . . .

Has there been a revolution?
Has he missed it?

Chopin hits the Gardens *molto-precipito* –

*

Give the man a welcome, a mobile and a hashtag –
keyboard-friendly fingers like his
deserve a touchscreen!

The blood I coughed up, soaked into
the rolled-out map of history.

We tweet our sympathy. Retweet.

The pogroms, the ghettos, the death camps . . .

We tweet the offer of a wall on Facebook.

My country has been torn apart again and again . . .

Almost midnight! Time for a glorious *en masse*
elevation of our smartphones:
we'll capture the fireworks showering
the Castle with coloured light.

My country disappeared as if it had never –

We'll put him on YouTube:
Celebrity composer Frédéric Chopin (1810-1849),
                                        tweeting
his thoughts about a Polish-style independence
                                        for Scotland.

I weep, how I weep –

We'll make the Hogmanay bells ring all year,
and Hogmanay kisses last forever.

Professor Peter Higgs' prediction of the particle that could almost be said to hold the universe together, was validated at CERN in Switzerland. The following year, he was awarded the Nobel Prize for Physics.

Professor Higgs Throws the Biggest Party Since the Big Bang

No alchemy at CERN, no sorcery, no spells –
particle acceleration only. Electron shells
stronger than our planet's gravity were split,
shattered . . . asked to spill
their treasure trove of *muons, strange* and *charm*.

Elementary, you might have said – until
Professor Higgs threw the biggest party since
the Big Bang!

4 July 2012.

At last, after millions, billions,
trillions of invitations Higgs boson shows up.
Shy, elusive, but statistically *there*.

At this, the CERN Collider and the universe itself
become as one. Whirling atoms
and the turning wheel of stars
stand integrated –

revealing Creation's utter certainty
and grace.

Dr. James Simpson [1811-70] and his colleagues experimented on themselves to discover a drug that would relieve the agonies that accompanied all surgery, particularly childbirth.

Sir James Simpson Sets Foot on a New Planet

Simpson's mother screamed and screamed and
screamed until –

Thirty-six years later the clock that measures out
human love and hope, human pain
and suffering as a beating heart,
a pulse, breath,

      slowed down . . .

           and almost . . .

                stopped

at the kitchen table of 52 Queen Street, Edinburgh,
4 November 1847

(   )

then started up again next morning. . .
                . . . less than a single tick later

when Simpson came to, lying tumbled
on his flag-stoned kitchen floor.

Recovered heartbeat, involuntary breathing,
a pulse –

Painless death, painless resurrection.

*

From outside there's the sound of rain battering
the darkness and an east wind
howling a path between the bare branches
and iron railings
of Queen Street Gardens.

In a previous world, his long-dead mother
has at last stopped screaming.

Simpson gazes round at the new
and so much kinder planet
that he's landed on.

'Chloroform! Blessed, blessed chloroform!'

Getting to his feet, he takes that first small step . . .

While walking on Salisbury Crags, James Hutton [1726-97]
came across rock formations that seemed to contradict Bishop
Ussher's accepted chronology of the world's creation in 4,004 BC.
Hutton, 'the Father of Geology', published his findings during
the years when the French Revolution was at its bloodiest.

James Hutton Learns to Read the Hieroglyphics of the Earth

Woken once too often by the *rattle-clatter*
of tumbril wheels on cobbles, the *click . . . click . . .*
click of distant knitting needles,
James Hutton decided never to go
to sleep again.

Then, by the light of several Edinburgh Council moons
(spares, in case the heavens were taken over
by the church), he tip-toed past storm-wrecked
Holyrood Abbey, went striding down
unimagined corridors,
through undreamt-of walls and doors where
Scottish Hope would one day
be cemented into place
(the bars across its parliament windows
wooden, just in case).

The Park . . . Salisbury Crags . . .

where several hundred million years ago,
the Earth had cracked itself wide open –

*

Detailed as a map of Man's undiscovered self,
zigzag Time lies flat-packed,
for everyone to see . . .

Stacked magma, olivine, dolerite chilled to glass,
eternity crushed to lines of slowly
spelled-out hieroglyphics, and cut
in blood-red haematite.

. . . and Hutton *sees it*. He's the first!

First to know he walks upon an ancient ocean floor
(God's Flood, the merest puddle in all *that* vastness).

First to hear the stone-hard heartbeat *pound-pound-
pounding* out Existence.

Elsewhere, Revolution has taken to the streets
with an accusation and a scream,
a guillotine-swish . . .
French clocks run backwards to Year One.

Sunday 23rd October 4,004 BC?
All in the blink of a biblical eye! says Hutton.

*

Meanwhile, you and I continue turning
on our axis to the *tick* . . .
tick . . . *tick* of Time that never
started *Once upon a* . . .
And will surely never, ever –

Ah, these strata, these infinities glimpsed between!

Tony Blair has sincerity stamped on his forehead, a brand name.
There is an uncanny resemblance to the finely sculptured eagle
glaring down at us from the plinth of the Melville Monument in
St Andrew Square, Edinburgh.

Tony Blair's Butterfly Effect

Having glided smoothly upwards –

Up...!
          And up..!
                  And up..!

Behold, Tony Blair standing where he should be –
poised sixty years and more above
the city of his birth.

Time enough for down-soft feathers to have stiffened
into archangel-strength wings,
time enough to curve himself a profile
of absolute conviction, take on
a gaze of stone-hard sincerity.

Set so high above the rest of us, he hears
God whisper to him,
personally.

Any moment now, the ex-PM might feel the need to stretch.

Beware!

Tony Blair's butterfly effect – when these wings beat,
distant city walls tumble,
men, women and children die.

Dame Elizabeth Blackadder is one of Britain's finest living artists.
Her meticulous work satisfies both traditional and contemporary
taste, restoring our faith in genuine creativity.

The Kinder Artist

Mornings unroll as unprimed, untrimmed canvas.
New-splashed colours drying out too soon
harden into lives.
Each city street's a portrait gallery we walk through.

God the Artist keeps himself well-hidden,
as well He might –
He has a lot to answer for.

Not just His recent winter palette
of sleet and rain, of day after day
slate-and-tenement grey . . .

but the casual painting-over of anyone
whose time, He likes to think,
is done.

*

Not so another artist, less ambitious,
and therefore kinder.

With her brushstroke sunlight yellows,
reds, vermilions, she offers flowers
(all in a moment's grace that could be
ours, if we allowed)
and cats who put us comfortably
in our place, knowing
they will outlive us.

Given their breathing-space of canvas,
Koi carp and kimonos are restored to life.

Hers is creation we can trust.

Remembering a Good Friend
(for Gavin W.)

No history but what we take for granted. Our lives are
as already read – and here's the writing on the wall.
We wrote it.

We always do.

No sanctuary for you till now.
All we shared seems all we'll ever know.

How can this be?
How can any of this be?

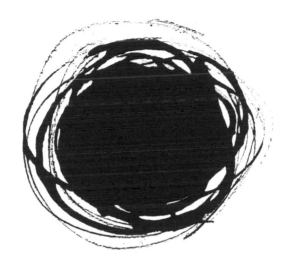

On 17 August 1513, a Scottish army of 30,000 men, made up of
conscripted farmworkers and labourers for the most part, was
assembled in Edinburgh to march down into England. With James
IV at their head, they ended up at Flodden.

A Gaitherin O Scottish Men

Scottish kings, Scottish lairds, chieftans, gentry . . .
No that mony gin they're coontit up –
a few score tae a generation.
Scotland's history, sae we're telt.

The likes o you an me? Fit-sodgers maistly,
mairchin . . . mairchin doon the years
whiles daein oor best tae no get killed
afore oor time.

Oor enemies? Ither kings, lairds, chieftans an gentry –
they'll rape oor wummen
an eat oor weans.
Sae we're telt.

*

King James is a guid an glorious king –
he daes things grand-style!

Holyrood Palace, re-biggin the Castle, stairtin up
the surgeons an the Navy.

He's sortit us oot grand-style tae –
Mons Meg hurlin daith a guid twae mile,
fower hunner ox tae puu the guns
an save oor strength
fer whit's tae come.

There's thirty thoosan o us gaithered here,
aa facin Sooth, an thoosans mair
tae whisky us
an bed us on the road . . .

At oor heid's a kingly king we'll mairch fer, kill fer,
dee fer if we hivtae!
Mairch aa the wey . . . an mair.

We're a richt-fou rantin roar o Scottish men, shair
this yince tae mak history fer oorsels –
a history that'll be oor ain!

My grandfather was severely wounded in the war, and there was a
great shortage of pain-relieving medicines. He suffered agonies in the
weeks that followed, only to die on the day peace was declared. This
poem was read during the BBC's WW1 commemoration programme.

My Grandfather Dreams Twice of Flanders

My grandfather dreamt he was trying hard to die
and no one would help him.
He dreamt he went walking across Flanders field,
and he saw the companies of dead men
whose screaming he still hears night after night.

The countryside was a woman dressed in red.
He saw her courted briefly by a million men
carrying bayonets and mortars – her face
turning towards his, turned his to stone
and made the white clouds whirl dizzily overhead.

My grandfather dreamt that he was six years old
and a woman decked in flowers or blood
was guiding him to Flanders field –

he saw ungathered poppies scattered on the floor,
and the ceiling tilting crazily,
and the lights swaying.
Shadows tumbling out of the darkness
beckoned him everywhere.

He saw her heaping flowers into a bed.
Then one by one she took the shadows
to lie with her, and one
by one he saw them disappear.

Robert Burns [1759-96] ended his life as a poet-cum-Customs and
Revenues officer in Dumfries which, like many Scottish towns,
enjoys a vigorous Planning Dept. and a road system that is being
constantly upgraded.

Robert Burns' First Poem For More Than 200 Years

Robert Burns' house was put on this earth
without planning permission –
no wheelchair access, fire doors!
No extractor fans!

For the next two centuries, intergalactic rubble
fell from the sky forming government buildings,
Planning departments. Administration.
Nearby, in St. Michael's kirkyard, the dead
rose from their graves to sit on committees,
consider applications and appeals.
Red and green men ruled the streets.

The River Nith silted up, and wept.

*

Today, fresh tar lapping its front steps,
and freshly-painted single, double,
triple yellow lines patrolling
its foundations, Burns' House knows
it's time to move on.

Avoiding anyone who tarmac our paths
into the future,
it navigates the one-way streets, No Entries
and contraflows.
Gatecrashes the ring road carouselling the town . . .

Accelerates into open country.

*

Robert Burns has long dreamt the moment
of his resurrection:
The first words of his first poem for more than 200 years
will be written in streaks of light
across the morning sky.

Creation waits to be renamed.

Rev. Alexander Peden [1626-86], also known as Prophet Peden,
was a leading figure in the Covenanter movement. A hunted man,
he preached in the open air and died while still on the run. The mask
and wig he needed as disguise can be seen in the National Museum
of Scotland.

Prophet Peden Rattles The Prison Bars Of The 21St Century

Long before the moment of his birth he'd climbed
a stone-slabbed stairway rising
from the planet's core.

The sometimes layered sometimes molten rock, was all
the certainty he knew and needed.
God's Word mapped out the darkness –
a braille of clustered minerals, crystals,
precious stones.

Emerging at last into daylight.

Entering this roofless church, the earth.

*

From his crow's nest of a pulpit, Prophet Peden scans
the perpetual ebb and flow of mountain,
glaciated valley, moorland
(eternity has no shore to break upon,
not here).

We've assembled under open skies as on
God's outstretched palm,
our skin flayed to rawness
by the Scottish wind and rain –

Raising his arms to the heavens, Peden drives us forward.
Forward! Forward!

Until . . . .

*

What unnamed continent is this? What century,
discovered upon whose unsteady palm (which might
at any moment clench into a fist,
to crush us all)?

As always, those who know are quick to tell us, quick
to help us navigate this ever-brand-new,
ever-better world.

We post our plans on Facebook,
tweet our feelings, our beliefs . . . Whatever.
We Favourite what matters most.
Retweet.

Our personal / professional /consumer profiles
are updated every hour.
We're LinkedIn, we're empowered!

Our enemies are quarantined safely
from our sight. Their severed nerves electrified.
The drowned are drowned over.

Guantanamo, Long Ketch, Auschwitz, Camp 16 ...

So many Calvaries to nail down conscience
on a daily basis.

We live in God's name, any god at all
whose blood flows thick enough
and black enough to serve
in the holy sacraments of Wall Street,
the Square Mile, Frankfurt, Beijing.

His litanies are the *Nikkei, Dax, Dow Jones ...*

*

Prophet Peden rattles prison bars that
only he can see –
invisible breeze-block walls
and locked doors
guard against the threat of freefall.

A Covenant – here?

And so, back to that ice-hardened winter afternoon,
late January 1686, the parish of Sorn.
Back to that frozen riverbank, trampled-grass path,
that dripping cave –

Stone bed / bracken pillow / God's stairway
leading him down . . . down . . . down . . .

While on convalescence at Craiglockart Hospital from wounds
sustained on the Western Front, Wilfred Owen [1893-1918] decided
to return to his company. He was killed a week before the Armistice.

Wilfred Owen Reads Between the Lines

Advance two steps / back two steps . . .
Breathless mouths get stopped with mud.
Advance two steps / back two steps . . .

*

Our generation's on the terrace sitting
the next dance out,
chairs lined up to catch the Scottish sun.

Below, a goods train trundles its clank of wagons
westwards into the future . . .

Then it's gone.

Edinburgh's at our feet. Because of railway soot
and chimney smoke, I can hardly see the Castle,
St Giles' Cathedral, Calton Hill.
How much clearer, the Forth Rail Bridge,
the coast of Belgium,
the distant fields of France . . .

The impossibly young nurse who heals
each wounded day, takes
my hand in hers.

Turns it over.

'These palm lines show,' she tells me, 'what
will surely . . .'

And how lightly she traces out the track
of each approaching bullet.
The smog-yellow drift of gas.
A mortar shell's sudden *THUD* full-stop.

There's barbed-wire laughter as the flesh
and muscle's ripped from
bloodied bone,
letting us clamber up to heaven.

A company of angels soaring
into the ever-blue –

Advance two steps / back two steps . . .
Breathless mouths get stopped with mud.
Advance two steps / back two steps . . .

This is a dance I know I will not live through.

All That We Have

Before I'd learned to speak I heard and saw only
what there was, and all there was
was enough.

So many years and so much understanding
later, I catch sight of you applying
a touch of lipstick, say,
or leaning forward to brush your red hair . . .

And the longing for all we cannot have
and all that we do have,
still overwhelms.

MAGIC FOR ALL

*The result of the Scottish referendum on Independence has ensured
that Trident remains based in Scotland. For the continued comfort
and security of us all, so we're told.*

Trident Mantra

Here's Fruit Juice raising the lid of our communal street bin.

ZOOM in on Edinburgh's most celebrated dosser,
his boots, overalls and multi-layered cape
(buttonless coat, windjammer jacket,
fleece) clambering in,
headfirst.

(His bicycle clutters the nearby pavement –
handlebars and frame a tangle of
broken-backed rucksacks, holdalls,
Tesco bags-for-life.)

He's choosing his new spring wardrobe?
A recliner for a long weekend?

The metal lid's slammed back down.

TRACK him wheeling away his property –
the ballast that helps him stay on course.

His streets, his bins, his treasure trove,
and all Edinburgh for a bed.

(Thanks to Face-Recognition Software, CCTV,
and Trident patrolling our dreams
to keep us safe, Scottish history is now updated
as it *actually happens.*
Living and dying is given *real* meaning.)

ZOOM in on those souvenir stigmata scars
across his palms. Silken-sleek, and gashed
the length of Garcloch every time
£20 billion and rising
slides into dock.

TRACK him. TRACK him to the next street,
to the next bin. TRACK his morning prayers.

TRACK the mantra that gets him through the day –

Vanguard. Victorious. Vigilant. Vengeance.

We live in a glass kingdom that seems each day to become more fragile. Should we worry? After all, our elders and betters are determined to take care of us.

A History of The Glass Kingdom

Back then, High Priests would breathe on every surface
of our sacred heart-stone,
lesser priests breathed
on the everyday transparency of streets,
buildings, billboards, trees, grass
and falling rain.

They breathed and they polished,
they made our precious kingdom shine!

(Beyond our borders lay a thanklessness
of darkness and division
where local deities clawed the sky,
stamped on the earth
to get attention.
Matters of life and death were settled
by divine clumsiness.

Small gods and smaller men – envy
gave them strength.)

Meanwhile, the light streaming from our
sacred heart-stone's core purified

and protected us.
Our dreams were forgiven,
our longings and regrets (the mess
of fingerprints we'd smear on whatever
we desired)
were painlessly erased.

Contented years, contented centuries. Until –

*

This morning, the sun has come to a standstill.
Beneath us, the permafrost contracts.
We feel it crack.
Feel it split.
Glaciers and polar icecaps are breaking off,
slipping (so distant from us, we hardly
hear a sound)
into the warming waters.

Our priests assure us they continue to breathe
and to polish every single moment
of every single day.

They say they breathe and polish harder
than ever before.

They have new incantations, they tell us,
new rituals.

Do they think they can move the sun?

*

Computer simulations show our kingdom
catching fire. Such an electronic crackling,
such a roar from the surround-sound speakers!

See-through roads and bridges melt.

Glass-hard girders buckle in the heat.

History's a sentence left forever
incomplete . . .

Victoria de Los Angeles was not only a celebrated singer . . .

The Composer's Cat

This cat we knew.
Alas, no longer now –
her chromatic rough-lick *mew*,
her mellow-modulated *meow*.

Armchair and bed preferred to floor,
or else, a stretched out belly-furred
lintel for an open door,
while feline micro-engine purred.

*

You morning-pawed to break night's spell
and wake another day.

And so your nine lives passed away.

Our thanks and greetings, and farewell,
Victoria LA.

The Darien Scheme of 1698 was Scotland's attempt at creating an international trading company to rival those of the English and Dutch. Speculation gripped the country, many rich and poor invested all their savings. They lost everything. Of the original 1,200 men and women who colonised the Isthmus of Darien, only a few survived. Had they been able to google Panama before setting out, much misery might have been averted. Perhaps.

Darien II

Real-time seems to pass too slowly?
Then defragment it.

If that doesn't work –

RUN a virus check.
QUARANTINE the Scottish gods who've hacked
into the system.

If that doesn't work –

- GOOGLE 'Financial Speculation:
  The Darien Scheme / Disaster, 1698'
- Print off each sorry A4 sheet
- Origami a fleet of paper boats
- Add 1,200 human lives for ballast
- Float the doomed armada 300+years into the past

UPLOAD the slurried, fever-ridden Panama swamps,
the gorged mosquitoes, the rats,

the snakes, the total lack of
anyone to trade with.
Most of all, the endless
tropical rain rain
rain and more rain.

UPLOAD the weight of Scottish gold
and silver coin (half the country's
hoarded wealth) stacked
and strongboxed on the nation's desktop
as on a green-baize gaming-table . . .

If that doesn't work –

SWITCH OFF at the mains and wait for 30 seconds.

REBOOT
Go to VIRUS VAULT
SELECT 'Scottish gods' and 'Unforgiveness'
Right-click both
DELETE

Meanwhile, Scottish history will have timed out.

REFRESH?

(Warning – Real-time does NOT repeat!)

The large and prominent clock of Edinburgh's Balmoral Hotel looks down the length of Princes Street, and is always set three minutes ahead. This is to speed up passengers who have trains to catch at nearby Waverley station.

Our Plea To The Balmoral Clock

Gazing down upon our all-too-human delay
of almost-joined-up city streets,
and a mortality that clearly
cannot be relied on,

you seem to promise us – what?

Do you feel the urgency behind our as-yet
unspoken words of love, the ache within
the gestures we lack courage
to complete?

Do you understand our need for hopes
and fears to free us
from the present moment?

If so, what we ask is this –

Let whatever time you show us
be our invitation into the future –

and a blessing on us all.

*Like art and religion before it, business enterprise now takes on
the responsibility to create the world we live in . . .*

Whatever Next?

Who hasn't dreamt of windfarms in Princes Street?
Strictly democratic, they'll brighten up our lives
electric-wise from Granton to Grange,
Jenner's to Poundland.

Just imagine –

fifty-foot high *maitre d's* perpetually
ushering us in to picnic
on the grassy slopes.

How the world will envy us!
How *Glasgow* will envy us!

It only needs a business plan.

Somewhere deep beneath the Castle, we'll have
a *terra-cotta* army standing guard,
as well it should.

McPyramids will house the future line
of Scottish pharaohs.

Ah yes, a business plan . . .

Wee Referendum Burd

See thon burbled chatter gaitherin
in the gloamin?

There's aye yin as canna git heard,
canna git sortit,
but keeps on joukin in an oot,
roun an aboot –

His sang's the name he'll caa hissel –
gin yince he sings it oot!

I love music and frequently work with composers and musicians. It's been my pleasure to produce the libretti for seven operas and numerous texts for orchestral and chamber pieces. Poets are often musicians manqué.

An Opera To Last A Lifetime

Before we ever learn to say –
we sing. Breathing song,
seeing-hearing-smelling-tasting-
touching everything-and-everyone song.

Then words come. Words mean.
Words weigh out what it is
we feel, what it is we do.
Who *we* are, who *they* are.

Separating what once was one
into here and there,
into now and then,
into theirs and yours and mine.

And so, if we would really live again,
if we would feel alive again –

Let's sing and sing and SING!

With our planet heading ever more rapidly towards self-destruct thanks to the tireless efforts of big business, governments and the like, it's about time someone came up with a plan.

How To Save The World

PART A

Question 1:
Please SELECT which best describes you:
DICTATOR / OLIGARCH / WARLORD (local) /
WARLORD (freelance) /CEO OF MULTINATIONAL
CORPORATION involved in energy production,
in the chemical or biotech industries, or in mass media /
WEAPONS MANUFACTURER or ARMS DEALER /
POLITICIAN (self-appointed or otherwise) /
BANKER/FINANCIER / TERRORIST
(freelance) / TERRORIST (affiliated) / OTHER

If you selected WEAPONS MANUFACTURER
or ARMS DEALER,
please proceed directly to PART B
Otherwise, go to question 2

Question 2:
Do you believe that YOU personally can save the world?
YES / NO / NOT SURE

If you selected YES, please proceed directly to PART B

Otherwise, go to Question 3

Question 3:
In the event of a nuclear, biological, chemical or terrorist attack, do you believe YOUR personal security is vital to the world's survival?
YES / NO / NOT SURE

If you selected YES, please proceed directly to PART B
Otherwise, go to Question 4

Question 4:
Are you prepared to do WHATEVER IT TAKES to save the world?
YES / NO / NOT SURE

If you selected YES, please proceed directly to PART B
If you have selected NO, or NOT SURE to questions 2–4, please proceed directly to PART D
Otherwise, go to Question 5

Question 5:
On a scale of 1-10, where 1 is NOT AT ALL CONFIDENT and 10 SUPREMELY CONFIDENT, how confident are you that the world can be saved by you ONLY?
1-2-3-4-5-6-7-8-9-10

If you scored 2 or less, please proceed directly to PART D
Otherwise proceed to PART B

PART B

From the drop-down menu, please SELECT
your current Real Time Location (RTL),
i.e. where you are now.

CONGRATULATIONS! You have selected 'COUNTRY X'

BREAKING NEWS – While you have been completing
PART A of this questionnaire, COUNTRY X has been
warned of a nuclear-biological-chemical-terrorist attack.
STATUS: IMMINENT

Please CHOOSE Username and Password
Please CONFIRM Username and Password

Please follow the link to –
www.howtosavetheworldfromitsenemies.com/
mypersonalsurvival

Please ENTER Username and Password
Please ENTER postcode of your RTL

The onscreen map indicates your nearest
Designated Safe Location (DSL).
Please proceed IMMEDIATELY to your DSL
for further instructions.
NOTE: Do not engage in conversation / explanation
with *anyone* before quitting your current RTL.

PART C

CONGRATULATIONS!
You have now reached your DSL.

ENTER Username and Password

When Door / Hatch / Manhole Cover / Other opens,
please proceed immediately inside.

NOTE: Door / Hatch / Manhole Cover / Other
will automatically lock behind you.
Do not be alarmed.
This is for your comfort and security.

Please find your WELCOME PACK.

You will remain in your DSL until advised to leave.
Enjoy your stay!

NOTE –
Feedback forms are included in your WELCOME PACK

PART D

THANK YOU.
You have successfully completed the questionnaire.

BREAKING NEWS – There is NO nuclear-biological-chemical-terrorist threat currently imminent. Self-selected enemies to world peace are already placing themselves in permanent detention.

When advised to do so, please feel free to begin celebrating. Then get on with your life.

CONGRATULATIONS!

Scottish Cat and Scottish Mouse

The very first *Because*
(no paws or claws
but logic's laws)
came once upon a mouse-click
slick as any electronic
tick ... tick ... tick ...
through Time's deleted *was.*

Binary YES and binary NO,
the cursor showing where to go
(its heartbeat is what matters most
to touchscreen lives
lived ghost-to-ghost).

But oh! Oh! OH!
that once upon a long ago
*cat*abatic flow
that's brought us from entropic high
to less entropic low!

Never mind the why and how
or need-to-know,
only that we've come at last
to *now* –
i.e. what this cat and mouse allow.

Scottish cat and Scottish mouse
play hide-and-seek about our house –
no walls, no floors,
no stairs, no doors,
and nothing in between,
just me and you and you and me –
our hopes for what will never be
our fears of what has never been.

While Scottish sun and moon and star
make us who and what we are,
all histories of this and that
are better left
to Scottish mouse and Scottish cat.

*First read at the House of Lords, this poem celebrates the
Authors' Licensing and Collection Society and its thirty-five
years' defence of authors' rights and moneys. A most noble and
valued institution!*

God Gives The Universe
A Second Shove

Thirty-five years ago God gave his most recent universe
the once-over – a reality check
on all those protons, neutrons
and electrons who'd gone their own sweet way
since that First Divine Shove.

How, He wondered, were things shaping up?

Empires and pyramids. Paperclips.
Plastic, McDonalds

Margaret Thatcher made Minister for Education!

Being omniscient, He knew even worse
was to come:
'pirate downloads' 'e-books'
'kindle' 'googled Chaucer' ,
and beneath that neo-verbal clotted spew
of Devil's spawn –
the Tomb of the Midlist Author.

. . . And so God wept.

God often weeps.
Often sighs,
then dries His eyes.

Then sleeps.

But in 1977, how could He settle back in heaven
when nations, unworthy of the name,
photocopied wholesale –
no second thoughts, no shame?

He'd heard of five-act plays,
of talks and stories that
were broadcast *gratis* worldwide –
no penny in the hat.

No *rouble, drachma, lira,* Thailand *baht*
came home to needy authors who
had grown papyrus pale-and-thin,
their royalties few

and far between. Live upon a publisher's advance?
Some chance!
Not copyright, but copy-*free*'d become systemic,
from backstreet press to academic.

Moved by sorrow, God then acted out of Love –
and gave the universe a Second Shove.

Holy finger raised on high
He wrote a message in the sky,
letters in fire. Their meaning? Anybody's guess –
A . . . L . . . C . . . S????

*

Fast forward to the present day,
this pleasure-land of politics at play
among the hedge funds,
where bailed-out bankers ease the strain
with extra magnums of champagne.

A threatened euro, falling pound?
Austerity the Master Plan?
– the logic's pitiless
and no more sound
than keeping food from a starving man!

When common sense has lost all clout,
art cut to the bone and the bone cut out,
the likes of me and you
must write our best, keep true.
Nothing else will do.

Afterwards we'll publish where we can,
then take our cue
from God –

We'll all give thanks, and bless
ALCS!

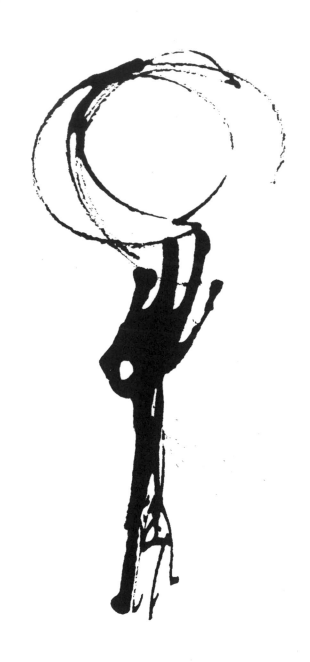

Scottish Independence As Seen From Above Edinburgh Castle

Standing an inch or two above Edinburgh Castle
I touch the sky for luck
(well, who wouldn't?)
and come away with history
smeared on my fingers.

Seems like Scottish history.

Hmm . . ., tastes like it, too!

With nowhere else to go, is this
where Scotland's past has ended up –
leaving us stranded in mid-air?

The wind's much stronger here, forever
blowing us a few days forwards,
a few days back.

Days, months, years . . .

One unexpected gust –
and we've been carried deep
into a Scottish Ice Age.

Our country's frozen into place
beneath us, preserved
in a centuries-thick glacier.

What now?

Should we wait until a tell-tale crack
opens at our feet, as if by magic?

Should we enjoy ourselves, get scarfed
and bunnetted to go sliding
Wheeeeeeee . . .
into the future?

One thing's for certain –
thanks to global warming we're sure to fall
back down to earth . . . and soon.

We'll have time to spread our wings?
To cross our fingers before
we hit the ground?

Prayer

When I reach the centre of the earth
let there be someone with me.
Each of us must bear the world's weight,
but not alone.

So when I return at last to this same hour
and this same place,
let there be someone raising even
the emptiness in their hands
towards me.

Note on the type

The Magicians of Scotland is set in
MVB Verdigris – a typeface designed
by Mark van Bronkhorst. It is a
Garalde text family for the digital
age and is inspired by work of
16th-century punchcutters Robert
Granjon, Hendrik van den Keere
and Pierre Haultin.